ANGELL

How Butterflies Get Their Wings

by Jean A. Hendrickson

Illustrated by Yon Chang
Based on sketches by Shirley A. Walsh

Dedicated to all special angels.

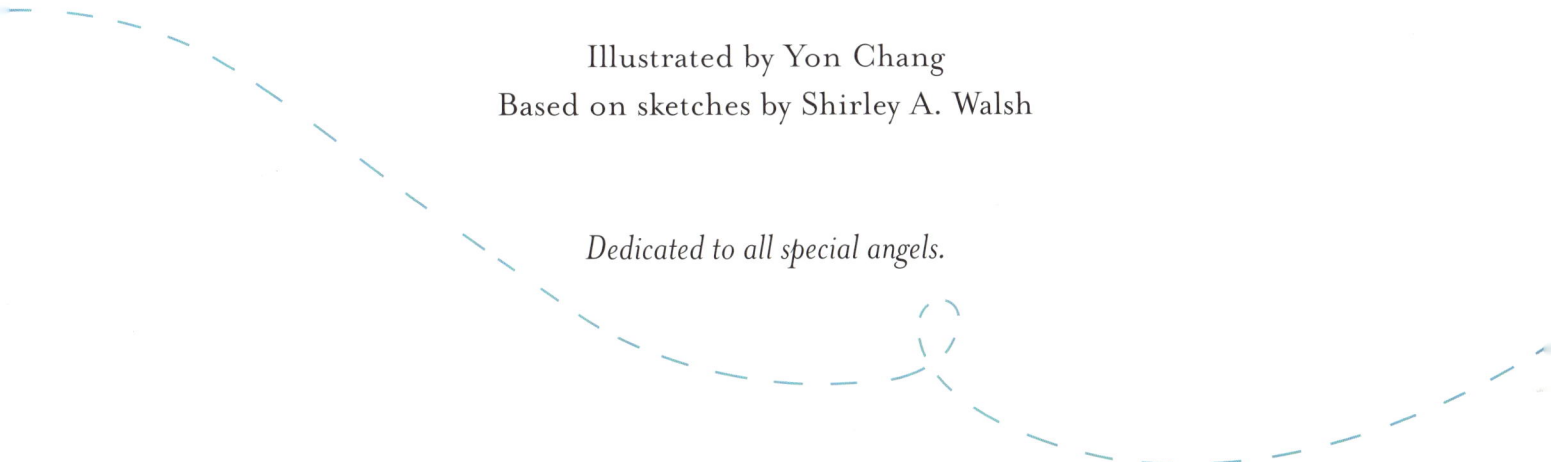

In the evening, as the stars were coming out, Angell would sit beside Angelbear and tell him of the WONDERFUL THINGS that happened when the world first began.

His favorite story

was about the butterflies and

how they got their BEAUTIFUL WINGS. Happily he would curl up

beside Angell and wait for her to start the story. Magic filled the air

when she began to speak.

"A long time ago the Elders – the oldest and wisest of the angels – and the WOODLAND FAIRIES worked together to fill the fields with bright flowers and the forests with mighty trees. Each morning the fairies gathered together to sing HAPPY SONGS about their beautiful world.

"One day the queen turned to the others and said, 'I think we have forgotten something. There is more work for us to do. Our fields are filled with flowers and our forests are filled with trees but what about the air above the fields and the forests? We have done nothing to make the air beautiful!' The fairies shook their heads sadly. It was true! Then they asked 'What can we do?' One of the fairies suggested they make PRETTY FLOWERS that could fly. Another fairy suggested they make tiny flying trees with LEAFY BRANCHES for wings and everyone laughed. The queen spoke again 'I know it will be hard to make the air beautiful but somehow we must find a way!'

"A few days later the fairies were busy working in the fields when they saw a COLORFUL CATERPILLAR sunning itself on a big green leaf." Angelbear spoke up, "I know what a 'pillar' is." (Angelbear had trouble saying caterpillar so he just called them 'pillars'.)

"It's a little worm with lots of colors and it has lots of TEENY TINY LEGS too." Angell nodded and went on with the story. "While the fairies were watching, a big puff of wind came by and blew the caterpillar right off the leaf. As it was falling, it reached out and grabbed onto another leaf that was blowing by. Together, SLOWLY AND GENTLY, the two floated down to the ground below.

"As they watched, an EXCITING IDEA came to the fairies. What if they gave wings to caterpillars and used their magic to teach them to fly? There were many caterpillars in the fields and forests. If this idea worked, they could give all of the caterpillars wings. The air everywhere would be filled with FLYING CATERPILLARS and the problem of making the air beautiful would be solved! Eagerly the fairies went to the Head Elder to ask for his help.

"An Elder listened to the fairies' ideas. He agreed that flying caterpillars would brighten the air above the fields and the forests and asked how they were going to make their plan work. A group of LITTLE ANGELS (the newest and smallest of all the angels) had been listening while the Elder and the fairies were talking. One of the little angels said, 'We could cut wings from the BRIGHT CLOUD MATERIAL found in the evening sunset!' Another little one suggested painting the wings with COLORFUL DESIGNS.

"The Head Elder thoughtfully stroked his beard and spoke to the fairies, 'Let our LITTLE ANGELS try their plan. Return to your forest. We will let the littleones make your wings.'

"The council of Elders was VERY PROUD of the little angels. They watched them make a wing or two and then gave them a WEE WORKSHOP of their very own where they could make and store wings.

"Happily the little angels went to work. Soon their idea for making wings turned out so good that there were stacks and stacks of BRIGHTLY PAINTED WINGS piled everywhere in the workshop. No one had stopped to think about finding the caterpillars or most of all, how could the little angels put wings on small VERY WIGGLY caterpillars?

"The fairies rushed to the workshop as soon as they heard about the pile-up of wings. They told the LITTLE ANGELS they would help them find the wandering caterpillars. However, the fairies soon learned that finding the CATERPILLARS was not the big problem but getting them to hold still for their wings was impossible. Everyone decided it was time to use FAIRY MAGIC.

DO NOT DISTURB

"Gathering in a circle, the fairies spoke the ANCIENT WORDS of their favorite spell. Immediately every caterpillar was helpless and under the fairies control. Like a robot each caterpillar started to build itself a COZY LITTLE NEST that the fairies later called a Cocoon after one of the words they used in their magic spell.

"When the cocoon was finally finished, each tired caterpillar slowly crept inside and fell into a deep MAGICAL SLEEP. It would not wake up until an angel gave it its' colorful wings and the spell was broken.

"While the caterpillars were sleeping in their COCOONS, work went on as usual in the wing workshop. The Elders suggested a SPECIAL GROUP to deliver the wings. This special group became the Wing Patrol."

Angelbear spoke up in a proud voice, "I'm the only bear on the WING PATROL. The Elders even gave me a patrol armband to show that I DELIVER WINGS too. It's so much fun finding all those 'pillars!"

Angell returned to telling the story. "The Elders made a SECRET DOOR in the back of the work-shop to help the WING PATROL find the cocoons. Caterpillars always hide them very carefully.

"It was a large golden door with a SHINY BRASS KEY. Beyond the door was a place called LOOK-OUT POINT. At Look-out Point the Wing patrol could see everything – everywhere. This made it easy to find a SLEEPING CATERPILLAR – no matter how care- fully the cocoon was hidden."

Angelbear sat up and
asked "Can I tell the
part where the sqwiggly
'pillars get their wings?"
Angell knew this was his
FAVORITE PART of
the story.

In his little bear voice Angelbear started to speak. "Most of the other angels just fly to their 'pillars but we like to make it a game!" He said, "Sometimes we float around on a FLUFFY WHITE CLOUD. Last time we used a rainbow for a giant slide and dropped right into Mrs. Brown's APPLE ORCHARD.

"We almost missed our 'pillar 'cause his cocoon was hidden behind a big red apple. You climbed the APPLE TREE while I stood watch so no one would see us.

"After you were up in the tree you did your toe wiggle and got REAL SMALL."

(One of the first things new little angels learn is the magic hidden in each big toe. A wiggle of the right toe to get smaller and a wiggle of the left toe to get bigger. TWO OR THREE WIGGLES and Angell was small enough to climb into a tiny cocoon.)

Angelbear spoke faster and faster as he continued with his story. "You carefully fastened the wings on the SLEEPING 'PILLAR and jumped down from the tree. Then we hid to see what would happen next. Soon there was a rustling noise and the cocoon started to shake. Whee, the MAGIC SPELL was broken and the sleepy critter woke up.

"Remember how it stretched its' wings and said, 'Oh, how beautiful they are!' Soon, after a couple of CAREFUL WAVES of the new wings, away it flew to join its' friends." Angelbear giggled as he remembered the stories the fairies told about the first few time the LITTLE ANGELS gave wings to caterpillars – the time before the Great Elder's Edict when caterpillars woke up, tripped over their wings and could only flutter around. The absentminded fairies had forgotten to add the FLYING PART to their magic spell.

Tired from telling his FUN STORY, Angelbear finished speaking. "Since our job was done and we had to get back to the workshop, we grabbed a ride on the PASSING WIND and in a twinkling we were back at Lookout Point.

"Angell, please tell me again about the wonderful Edict of the Elders. You tell it better than anyone else." Angelbear snuggled down beside Angell. The room became quiet and the air filled with a soft warm glow as she began to speak. "At the beginning, the Elders CAREFULLY WATCHED the work of the little angels and the fairies. When they saw how lovely the winged caterpillars were, even though they didn't really fly, they met in council to decide what they could do to be a part of this WONDERFUL PLAN.

"The GREAT ELDER rose and spoke to the council. 'These flying caterpillars are truly a wonderful sight,' he said. 'We need a SPECIAL MIRACLE to honor our little ones and the fairies.'

"Raising his arms toward the sky, the Great Elder called out to the powers of nature to hear him – and to grant him his wish for a miracle. Suddenly a bolt of lightning shot across the sky and a POWERFUL VOICE thundered out about them.

'Great Elder, Thy wish has been granted! From this time on, when a caterpillar gets its' wings, a Miracle will come to pass! LITTLE ANGELS must forever deliver wings to sleeping caterpillars but then – Behold! It will be a BUTTERFLY that awakens to spread its beautiful wings and fly away! So shall it be! I have spoken and my word is law!'"

As Angell finished the story, a hush fell over the room. The stars outside their window were SHINING EVEN BRIGHTER than before. A shooting star streaked across the sky. It made a PERFECT ENDING for this timeless old story. Angell reached out and hugged Angelbear.

Quietly she said "That is the way it has been, Angelbear. Not only does a caterpillar change into a BEAUTIFUL BUTTERFLY while it is sleeping but when it awakens from it's magic sleep, it doesn't remember that once it was a caterpillar that didn't even know how to fly."

Angelbear rubbed his LITTLE ROUND EYES and started to yawn. It was getting late and he was very sleepy. Angell picked him up and gently tucked him in bed. As she turned out the light, the room filled with the soft glow from the stars. Over Angelbear's soft bear snores Angell whispered, "SWEET DREAMS ANGELBEAR AND SWEET DREAMS TO ALL OF YOU!"

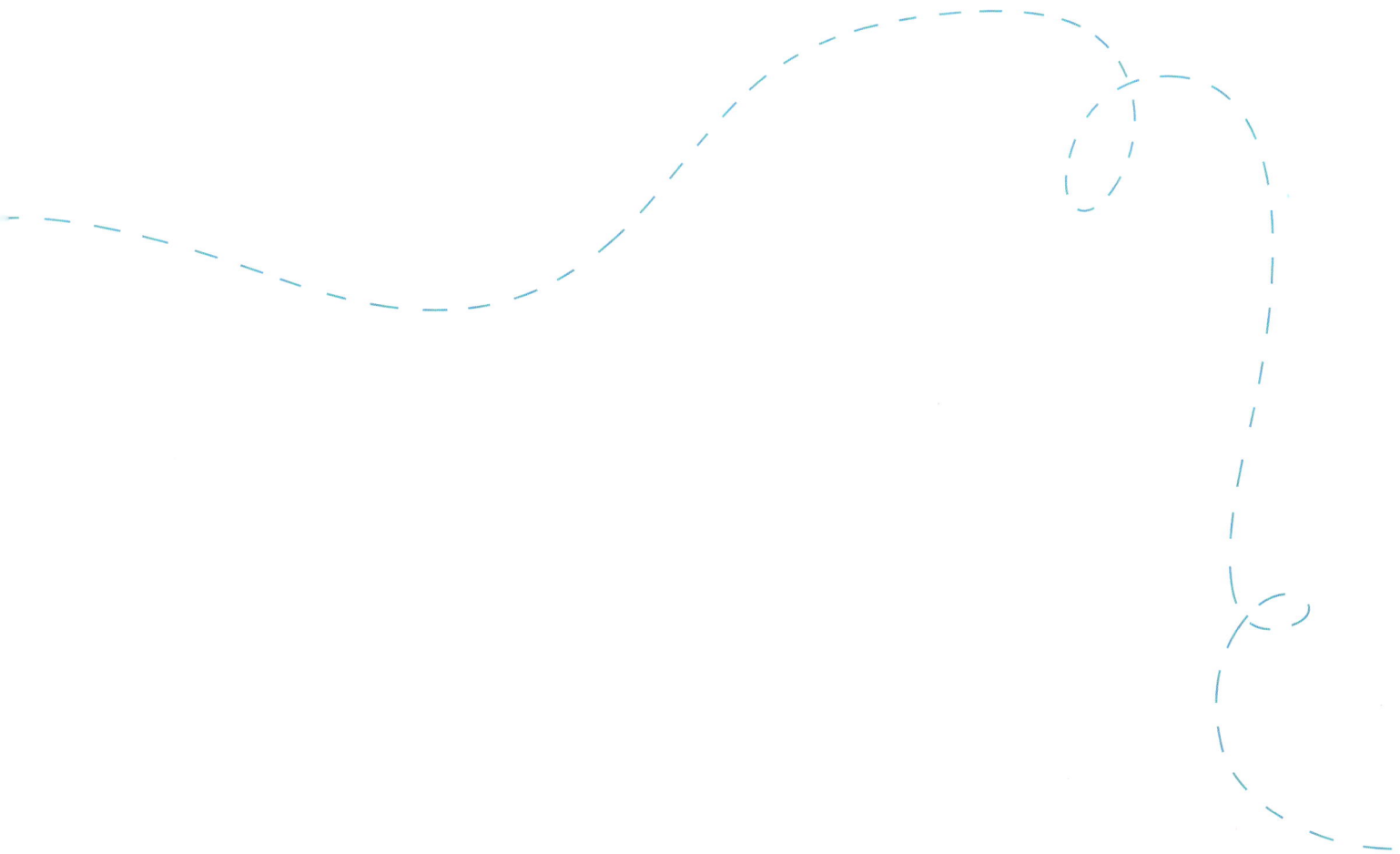